AF504427

HELP!
My Kid Won't Go to School!

Finding Hope on a Bad Day

Katie Fowle & Sharoya Ham

FLOURISHING FAMILIES PRESS

Help! My Kid Won't Go To School

© 2023 by Katie Fowle and Sharoya Ham

Published by Flourishing Families Press

ISBN: 979-8-9901297-1-9 (softcover)

ISBN: 979-8-9901297-0-2 (ebook)

Dedication

Katie

To my daughter, who taught me to be the mom she needed me to be and to love doing it.

Sharoya

To my former students whose challenging behavior taught me so much.

Acknowledgments

- To Malachi Ham, thank you for giving us the questions we needed to ask each other before agreeing to coauthor this book. It turned our friendship into a sacred partnership.

- To the hero of this book, thank you for allowing us to share your story so parents around the globe could know how to be the parents their children need during this season of their lives.

- To our beta readers, thank you for your valuable feedback. Jennie, Barbara, Christy, Diana, Kary, Ben, Matt, and Teri, we're happy to say we agree with all your recommendations. This finished book exists because of your input.

- To Lauren Wells, thank you for providing your voice and wisdom in the Foreword. It provides a beautiful entry into our book.

- To Elizabeth Trotter, thank you for your patience and diligence in editing this book and coaching us through the process.

Contents

Foreword

When speaking to crowds of parents at schools around the globe, I often think (and sometimes even say), "If you hear nothing else, hear this:

The health of the parents directly impacts the health of the children. And there is almost always more to the story of your child's behavior than what you can see."

In working with hundreds of families through TCK (Third Culture Kid) Training and Unstacking Company, school refusal regularly rises to the top of the list of most stressful challenges for a parent to deal with. It is a challenge that grows quickly and furiously, spiraling steadily into a situation where the child feels unheard and misunderstood, the parent fights or surrenders, and the child still doesn't attend school. As the number of missed school days increases, emotions heighten, and a battle wages between the parent and the child. Often the parent and their co-parent have different strategies for how the battle against school refusal could be won.

As you'll find throughout this book, the solution is not to fight harder, and the enemy is not your child.

The solution is looking inward at how school refusal impacts you, assessing how your behavior is helping or hindering the process, and recognizing that the battle will only be won through careful examination of the people, places, and events affecting your child. Then, you can look more deeply into your child's inner world and compassionately investigate the deeper reasons behind school refusal. Discovering those deeper layers gives you and your child a common enemy to fight – either with new skills or some strategic changes.

In these pages, you'll find hope. You'll see through the stories woven throughout that you're not alone and that there is a path forward. You probably picked up this book because of school refusal, but what you'll gain through humbly reading and reflecting through these pages will impact so much more than that. The journey this book will take you on will strengthen your relationship with your child and give you tools for navigating any range of conflicts that arise.

So, thank you on behalf of your child for putting in the hard work that will help you to be the parent your kid needs and for doing the deep work that will ultimately get them out the door and off to school.

By Lauren Wells,
author and CEO of TCK Training and Unstacking Company

Introduction

School refusal is frustrating, confusing, and exhausting. It makes sense to want to throw blame at your child or others when school refusal arises. And unlike with other parenting challenges, there aren't many books, experts, or resources to help you know what to do.

School refusal isn't your child's fault. It isn't your fault either. Instead, school refusal is life's way of saying, "Slow down. Your child needs you. They need you to show up in different ways than they've needed you before."

In this book, we'll show you how school refusal is the complex interaction of multiple factors in your child's life and how small tweaks in your parenting can help your child get back to school.

The reality is that you can't drag your kid to school. And sometimes, no amount of verbal or emotional feedback can make them change their behavior. What you can do, however, is surrender to your own process of personal growth as a parent. Easy? Definitely not. It will require you to grow your parenting skills. But as these new skills develop, you'll begin to see positive changes.

This book is a nudge – to you, not them. It gives you a plan of how to make small changes to achieve three goals:

- You show up as the parent your child needs you to be today.

- Your child goes to school! Finally!

- Your family begins to thrive again.

If you have a spouse, co-parent, or another person helping to raise your child, we strongly recommend inviting them to work through this book with you. They are vital to the process.

Your situation may look bleak right now, but in the end, you will see both your child's growth and your own.

We created this book to help you move:

FROM	TO
Confusion	Clarity
Threats and yelling	Supportive boundaries
Distant relationships	Stronger bonds
Your child not attending school	Your child attending school

We've been in your shoes and have successfully coached other parents through their child's school refusal.

You can do this! We can do this!

Take it one step at a time.

CHAPTER 1

Getting to Know Our Stories

Meet Katie Fowle, M.Ed

Hi, I'm Katie. I have been an educator for over twenty years and am today the proud mom of two daughters, a tween and a teenager. In my private tutoring practice, Learning to Flourish, I help my students overcome academic challenges caused by dyslexia and ADHD. Every day, I watch my students go from feeling shame and discouragement to having the confidence they need to succeed in school.

In 2021, my parenting journey got a serious flat tire. My daughter refused to go to school, and I just didn't know what to do! I felt embarrassed, angry, and confused about how to help her. When the behavior continued, I began to feel total despair.

Throughout my daughter's life, I believed I had done all the right things, read all the right books, and practiced all the right parenting skills. To be honest, I think I was a bit of a know-it-all. How could I not know how to parent my child?

But guess what? I didn't know what to do when my daughter refused to get out of bed and go to school, and neither did my husband.

We blamed one another and had constant fights about how to parent. Eventually, I realized that my husband and I parented very differently. We weren't on the same page about our own parenting and didn't know how to get there. I gave in to my daughter's moods and demands, whereas my husband became harsh and punitive. And this difference in approach wasn't helping to get our daughter to school.

My daughter is the hero of this book. She is determined, brave, and never gives up. Her determination teaches me to be passionate in life. Her bravery motivates me to feel my emotions. Her willingness to never give up inspires me to overcome my daily challenges.

My daughter is the hero of this book because she is a hero to me. She permitted me to share our intertwined story because she wanted our story to help other kids.

Here's what I wish someone would have told me when I was trying to stop school refusal in its tracks.

Stop the blame game - it doesn't work and creates more suffering.

Take one step at a time - there's no quick fix; it will take time.

Accept what is - some days may not turn out how you want.

Be patient - your child needs you to be calm and consistent.

Have faith - do what you need to keep your spirits up.

It's been two years since school refusal became an issue in my home. I tried a lot of things to make it go away. Eventually, my family sought help from a therapist trained in Dialectical Behavioral Therapy (DBT). Things finally began to get better.

I recognize all parents may not have access to DBT. That's why I wanted to write this book. I want to share what I learned from DBT therapy so you get the benefits without going to appointments.

I'm happy to report that school refusal no longer dominates our mornings. On the rare occasion when it does happen, I remember to remain calm, clearly communicate, and stay consistent with natural consequences.

NOTE: If your child is depressed, suicidal, using drugs, or has an eating disorder, please seek mental health support before implementing the strategies in this book. These disorders are beyond the scope of this book. However, we highly recommend Dialectical

Behavioral Therapy (DBT) for children and their families dealing with these disorders. See the Appendix for helpful resources.

Meet Sharoya Ham, M.Ed.

Hi, I'm Sharoya, a reformed school-resistant child. I wish my parents had access to this type of how-to book forty years ago. It would have saved them and me from a lot of frustration.

As a child, I did not respond well to situations that made me anxious. The problem wasn't that I didn't want to go to school. Rather, I didn't know how to express what I was feeling.

If I did, perhaps I would have said something like:

- My stomach hurts. I think I'm nervous about my test today. I'm scared to go to school.

- I feel extremely sad. You guys (my parents) were arguing last night. I don't want to go to school. I want to hide.

- I am embarrassed by how I look. My self-esteem is low. I would rather stay home where it feels safe.

- I am moody, and I don't know why. I think I'm depressed. It feels like a weight on me. I don't enjoy anything, especially school. I want to die.

Thankfully, I now know how to express myself after many years of therapy. If only I had learned more coping skills earlier, I might have saved some money! But the good news is that my childhood challenges have fueled my passion for helping parents succeed at being the parents their children need them to be.

For the past decade, I've worked as an International Parent Coach. I share the secrets I've learned as a mom, teacher, and behavior specialist with families around the globe through my parent-coaching practice, Embrace Behavior Change. My graduate degree is in Applied Behavior Analysis. But let me tell you, no academic curriculum taught me more about managing adolescent behavior than my 150 at-risk Algebra 1 students that I taught in 1999. (Yes, I remember the year!)

It was my hardest year of teaching. They cursed; they came late; they threw tantrums. I often left work feeling like a total failure. But I kept trying to figure out what they needed to succeed in my class. They taught me how to talk to them, what to do, and what not to do to get them moving in the right direction. And now, I teach my clients what they need to say and do to help their children.

In each chapter of this book, I provide you with parent coaching in real time. You will receive step-by-step guidance, thought-provoking questions, checklists, and scripts.

Parents often ask me, "Do you believe in a firm approach to parenting?" I do. A firm approach is fine as long as it works and is not degrading.

A parent once asked me, "How will my child know I'm in charge if I'm not stern?" My answer was, "Do what great teachers do." They remain calm, respectful, yet firm.

Some parents may find the words in the scripts too soft. That's ok. I encourage you to replace them with other positive words.

A Word of Caution

Successfully addressing school refusal requires a lot of communication between parents and their children. We realize that some parent-child relationships are tense. Communication might be minimal or even volatile. If this is your situation, know that there is hope. Families with strained relationships transform in ways they never could have imagined before engaging in therapy or parent coaching. It's okay to reach out for professional help if you need it.

Problems are unavoidable, and sometimes life just gets messy. It's essential, however, to lean on others during these moments.

Will This Book Work for You?

We realize particular sections of the book apply to only some children. Yet we are 100% sure there's a chapter, section, or poignant sentence that will propel you forward and move you closer to a solution. So we encourage you to skip around and take from the book what you need.

No book or program will make school refusal disappear like magic. School refusal does not go away fast. It's a process.

We will show you how to connect with your child. As you do so, you'll see why events like school refusal are perfect opportunities for developing your child's life skills.

Finally, remember that we are here for you. We will support you through this process.

CHAPTER 2

What's Your Story?

This book is filled with stories. But before you read any further, we want you to grab a pen and write your story on the Reflection page at the end of this chapter. It will be your baseline before and after reading this book. It will show you how far you and your child have come!

Next, you'll answer an important question.

Your answer to this question will help you on the hard days when you want to give up. It encapsulates your ultimate long-term goal and will serve as your compass on this journey.

REFLECTION

1. Do you know why your child is struggling? If so, explain.

____

____

____

____

2. How do you feel about your child's school refusal?

____

____

____

3. What feelings do you think your child is dealing with?

____

____

4. Have you considered getting professional support for your child?

———————————————————————

———————————————————————

———————————————————————

5. Have you considered getting professional support for yourself?

———————————————————————

———————————————————————

———————————————————————

We want you to complete the prompt below using "mindless writing." It's the quickest way to quiet the thoughts in your mind so you can find out what your heart is "thinking."

1. Set a 30-second timer.
2. Close your eyes.
3. Write without lifting your pen for the entire duration.

Prompt:

When your child turns 30, what do you want them to say about the way you responded to them during their bout with school refusal?

"My mom/dad......."

CHAPTER 3

Quick Facts About School Refusal

Each parent reading this book has a different story. Yet every reader has the same goal: to get their child to attend school without a hassle! Before we give you practical steps to deal with your child's resistant behavior, we want you to understand some basic facts about school refusal.

What is School Refusal?

School refusal, a term coined by educators, psychologists, and other professionals, refers to the avoidance of a child attending school or persistent difficulty staying in the classroom throughout the day.[1] Unlike truancy,

---

[1] https://www.ncbi.nlm.nih.gov/books/NBK534195/

school refusal behavior does not include skipping class or ditching school.[2] Instead, school refusal behavior may look like a child refusing to get out of bed in the morning, complaining of headaches or stomach aches, or acting defiantly.[3]

Why Does School Refusal Occur?

Common reasons for school refusal include:

Emotional & Mental Health Issues

Some kids struggle with their mental health and cannot escape from thoughts of anxiety and depression, which can lead to eating disorders, drug use, and thoughts of suicide, making it extremely difficult to function at school.

Avoidance Issues

Some kids experience situations they fear or want to avoid at school. Here are some examples[4]:

- Learning difficulties
- Bullying
- Returning to school after a break or illness
- Having to get up early
- Being bored at school
- Not seeing the value of school
- A parent being hurt while they're at school

---

[2] https://schoolavoidance.org/school-avoidance-vs-truancy/
[3] https://www.psycom.net/anxiety/school-refusal
[4] https://www.ncbi.nlm.nih.gov/books/NBK534195/

Feeling Bored by School

Teaching kids how to get unbored is an essential life skill. When their grades are in jeopardy, they can't afford to disengage and use boredom as an excuse. They must see boredom as an opportunity to ask themselves, "What can I do to refocus so I can succeed?" Take a look at the "Get Unbored" list in the Appendix for practical ways your child can reignite their connection with school.

Needing More Agency Over Decisions

Parent-child relationships can get really tense during the adolescent years as maturation occurs and adolescents' natural desire for independence increases. It's important to recognize the transition from childhood to independence is developmentally *necessary*.

Stressful life changes such as divorce, remarriage, or relocation can cause your child to want more control over their lives. You may see an increase in irritable, rude, or defiant behavior. Your child might resort to excessive gaming or withdrawal from interactions with the family.

Some adolescents may think, "If I can't get my way, I'm going to show my parents who's in charge!" School refusal is one way they can exert some control. This may seem like total manipulation. But in actuality, the defiant behavior is the child's way of saying, "I feel unheard, overlooked, and misunderstood. I'm going to push people away to see if they even care about my feelings, opinions, or *need* for more ability to make decisions."

It's normal to want to clamp down, but the first step to take is to pull back from expressing your opinions, verbal reprimands, and threats. It's time to go quiet and create a connection before correction. This will be extremely hard to do in the face of resistance, but it's a prerequisite for turning your situation around.

See resources in the Appendix for building stronger bonds and managing excessive gaming.

When Is School Refusal Likely to Appear?

School refusal commonly appears when children change schools, towards the beginning and end of the school year, after a death, illness, or a move, or during any other major transition. The problem is more severe in older children than in younger children.[5]

How Long Does School Refusal Generally Last?

The problem of school refusal is *chronic*. Chronic doesn't mean hopeless. It simply means that children who resist attending school or staying in class will struggle for an extended period. School refusal episodes, however, will reduce in frequency and intensity over time with an effective intervention plan.

How Can Parents Keep It Together When They Are Ready to Explode?

It's human to be annoyed, angered, disappointed, irritated, and downright mad when nothing you do is

---

[5] https://www.nasponline.org/

working. However, these intense feelings only make your child feel bad and worsen the situation.

The good news is that studies show parents can successfully coach their children through school refusal.[6] This book will show you how.

We want to reiterate: If your child is depressed, suicidal, using drugs, or has an eating disorder, please seek mental health support before implementing the strategies in this book. These disorders are beyond the scope of this book. However, we highly recommend Dialectical Behavioral Therapy (DBT) for children and their families dealing with these disorders. See the Appendix for helpful resources.

---

[6] https://developingchild.harvard.edu/science/key-concepts/resilience/

REFLECTION

Which of the following issues relates to your child?

- ☐ Emotional & mental health
- ☐ Avoidance
- ☐ Feeling bored by school
- ☐ Tense parent-child relationship
- ☐ Stressful life events: divorce, remarriage, moving, death
- ☐ Excessive gaming
- ☐ Other ___________________________

Notes:

____

____

____

____

____

____

CHAPTER 4

Are You Fanning the Flames & Don't Know It?

In Chapter 3, you reflected on possible reasons for your child's school refusal. Now, let's look at ways you may be reinforcing your child's school refusal behavior and not know it.

☐ Has your child's school recommended an educational evaluation, and you haven't followed up because you want to protect your child from being labeled?

☐ When your child stays home from school, are they allowed to use screens, go outside, spend time with you, play with their pet, lie in bed, visit friends after school, or do other enjoyable activities because you want to keep them occupied?

☐ Have you been working to solve school refusal independently without reaching out to your child's teachers or guidance counselor, family members, and friends to ask for support because you feel like you should know how to solve the problem?

☐ Does your child have emotional or behavioral outbursts or an eating, drug, or other addictive disorder, and you haven't sought help from your child's pediatrician or other certified health care providers because you are nervous?

☐ Do you try to comfort your child by allowing them to stay home when they are anxious or depressed because it hurts to see them suffer?

☐ Are you providing written excuses for your child when they miss school due to school refusal because you don't want them to fail or get suspended?

☐ Has your child been grieving a move, divorce, or death for a while, and you've stopped providing validation or support?

☐ Do you allow your teen to spend lots of time alone

in their room with little to no engagement with the family because you want to keep the peace?

☐ Is your schedule so busy that you find it hard to make time for enjoyable moments with your child even though you want to?

If you checked one or more of the items on the list, we know your intentions are well-meaning. However, these actions are counterproductive. They reinforce school refusal behavior.

So here are three things you can start doing right away:

Seek professional help where needed. Contact your child's teacher for an educational evaluation, a pediatrician, or a therapist for mental health support.

Turn off the internet when your child stays home from school. Home should be the least desirable environment possible. Turning off the internet and collecting screens will ensure your home is boring.

Let the school know what's happening. Covering up your child's absences doesn't allow your child to experience the natural consequences of not attending school. Deterrent consequences include grade retention, summer school, detention, exclusion from make-up work, removal from after-school activities, etc.

It's important to let your child receive unexcused absences for their school refusal. This allows your child to experience consequences beyond your home.

Most students start to get nervous when they risk being retained. We know that watching your child jeopardize their future is hard and scary. However, as parents, we must think long-term.

Remember, you are raising an adult. Would you want your child to depend on you in their twenties to get them out of bed or go to work? If your answer is no, then now is the time to let them fail so they can learn the correlation between their actions and natural consequences.

Natural Consequences

We use the term "natural consequences" throughout this book, so we want to be clear about what they are and aren't.

Natural consequences are not threats, nor are they created on a whim. They are predetermined reactions to specific behaviors. These reactions can be rewarding or deterrent.

For example, let's say your child is looking forward to a field trip at school.

The teacher communicates that students must arrive at school on time to attend the field trip.

If your child gets to school on time, they go on the field trip. This is a rewarding consequence of their behavior.

On the other hand, if your child misses the bus because they didn't wake up on time, and you hold your ground by not rushing them to school, then they don't get to go on the field trip. This is a deterrent consequence to their behavior.

When you allow for natural consequences, both rewarding and deterrent, you teach your child that their behavior can have pleasant or aversive consequences. More importantly, they learn that they have control over their choices and the outcomes of their decisions.

REFLECTION

Are you fanning the flames and don't know it? Look at the checklist on page 23 again, and make note of the ones that apply to you.

What actions are you committed to taking within the next seven days?

☐ Seek professional help where needed (see Appendix).

☐ Let the school know what's happening.

☐ Collect screens when your child refuses school.

☐ Other (explain).

CHAPTER 5

Getting Unstuck

I(Katie) could feel the frustration rise in my throat. It was another morning, and my daughter wasn't attending school. Again. My chest tightened as the clock ticked past 8:45 a.m. I watched other neighborhood children head to school.

I wanted to get my daughter out the door by any means necessary. The rage I felt scared me.

My husband frequently traveled for work, so I was often alone, trying to get our daughter to school in the mornings. And when my husband was home, we weren't on the same page.

I believed our daughter needed us to be more empathic and encouraging. In contrast, my husband was confident that our daughter needed us to be stern and give more harsh consequences.

Neither of these approaches worked to get our daughter out of bed and off to school.

That morning, I just couldn't take it anymore! And that's when I reached out for help.

Dialectical Behavior Therapy (DBT) provided the answers I needed. DBT was hard work, and the most challenging work I had to do during my DBT process was to accept that it was no one's fault.

But I soon learned I could change the situation by changing how I reacted.

If you are reading this book, I suspect you can't take it anymore either. You are probably wondering:

- How am I supposed to keep my job/other commitments when my child isn't going to or staying in school?

- I don't want to go to jail for dragging my kid to school. What am I supposed to do??

You might have these thoughts because school refusal is incredibly stressful and confusing.

Parent Coaching in Real Time

To solve the problem of school refusal, you must understand the nuances behind your child's resistance. Have you ever wondered why your child is resistant some days and not others?

It's because the triggers causing their avoidant behavior aren't always present. In this book, we refer to triggers as situations or environments that prompt negative emotions and which result in school avoidance.

Here are some examples that might trigger certain emotions:

- Having to get up early prompts anger.

- Listening to an uninteresting lesson prompts boredom.

- Engaging with irritating teachers or peers prompts frustration.

- Being alone at lunch or during breaks prompts loneliness.

- Hearing hurtful comments or receiving stares prompts sadness.

- Learning of mass shootings prompts fear of dying or a loved one dying.

- Being unprepared for a class prompts feelings of worthlessness.

- Having panic attacks prompts a debilitating cycle of anxiety.

- Watching domestic violence prompts concern for parent's safety.

- Being "different" (ethnicity, language, new student, learning difference, physical difference) prompts many emotions.

Before we help you look for solutions, we want to ensure you understand your child's triggers.

- What are they?
- When do they occur?
- How do they alter your child's mood?
- How does your child feel physically when triggered?

Direct conversation isn't always helpful when you're starting to uncover your child's triggers. A question like, "What's causing you not to go to school today?" may elicit a door slam or a "You just don't get it!"

But you are going to learn a secret weapon: the indirect conversation.

Here are a few ideas to help you uncover your

child's triggers through an indirect conversation. We hope they will assist you in creating your own strategies.

Ask a family friend to help you investigate. Your child will likely tell them more than they will tell you.

1. How's school going?

2. What's your favorite class? Why?

3. What class is your least favorite? Why?

4. If you could create the perfect school for yourself, how would it differ from the school you are in now?

Chat with teachers to better understand what your child is experiencing throughout the day.

1. How would you describe my child's mood in your class?

2. Have you noticed any academic or social challenges?

Table Talk. Plan a family meal where *everyone* must answer:

1. What was the funniest part of your day?

2. What was the worst?

3. What are you not looking forward to at school/work?

4. What part of your day do you wish would happen again tomorrow?

5. Why do you like your job/school? Explain.

Put distance between you and your words. Write a note or text instead of conversing with your child in person. See if it stimulates conversation. But don't force it.

1. I noticed yesterday you came home happy, and today, you seemed a bit down/frustrated/angry. I'm here to listen if you want to talk about it.

2. I know you were nervous about your test today. I hope you are proud of yourself for having the courage to show up! Would you like to go to the movies to celebrate?

REFLECTION

Before moving on to Chapter 6, decide which two investigations from the list above you will do *and* when you will complete them. It's important to keep yourself accountable by setting deadlines.

Which two investigations will you conduct?

- ☐ Ask a family friend to help you investigate.

- ☐ Chat with teachers to better understand what your child is experiencing throughout the day.

- ☐ Have a Table Talk.

- ☐ Put distance between you and your words.

- ☐ Other_________________________________

I will complete investigation #1 by _________________________.

I will complete Investigation #2 by _________________________.

Notes:

____

____

CHAPTER 6

Taking the First Step

I (Sharoya) can still recall how awful I felt about attending school whenever I had a test, book report, or project due.

I felt like I would rather die than go to school. I don't remember telling my parents how I felt. I'm sure it never crossed their minds to ask. That's just not what parents did.

I now know that those overwhelming feelings of fear and dread could be summed up as one word: anxiety. At ages seven, twelve, or even sixteen, I did not have the words to say, "I feel anxious" or "I think I'm not feeling well because I'm scared to take my test." I simply did whatever I could to stay home on those days.

School refusal behavior is often easy to identify: staying home, refusing to get out of bed, faking illnesses, and skipping class. Uncovering your child's underlying triggers and why they avoid school is more complex.

In chapter 5, you started to gather insight into what might be causing your child's school refusal through indirect conversation. Now it's time to set a calm atmosphere and listen with fresh ears so you can learn more about your child's potential triggers for not attending school.

Parent Coaching in Real Time

Remind yourself of your compass (page 16). School refusal is temporary, but your response to your child during this challenging time will leave a lasting impression. You have the power to determine whether it will be positive or negative.

Set a friendly atmosphere. Catch your child when they are in a good mood. Talk to them when no one else is around. Be sure to smile as you talk.

Say:

> "Hey Buddy, I want to chat with you after dinner for 15 minutes. When we talk, you can set a timer. I promise I will finish the conversation when it rings. I'll see you after dinner. Alright?" *Don't let them know what the conversation is about. Let it be a tease.*

Share your story. Connect with your child by telling them about you.

Say:

> "Sweetie, in middle school, I hated my English class." (Share why, how it made you feel, and what you wish your

parents or teachers would've done or known.)

"I see that you aren't enjoying school. Tell me, what do you wish I would do differently to make getting up and going to school less stressful? What would you like the school or your teachers to change to make school enjoyable?"

OR

"Sweetie, I was a total nerd in school. LOL! There wasn't a day I didn't want to go to school. I realize, however, that everyone isn't as weird as me. When I see you not wanting to attend school, I struggle to understand your feelings. So, I have two questions: What do you wish I would do differently to make things less stressful? What would you like the school or your teachers to change to make school enjoyable?"

Listen with fresh ears. Take in what your child says. Pay attention to their facial and body moments.

- Don't try to solve the problem during this conversation. Simply listen and ask additional curious questions until the bell rings.

- You could also say, "Let me know if I understand you correctly. You're feeling like you hate school because…… and this is causing you to feel……"

- End by saying, "Thank you for helping me better understand. I will think about everything you said, and I will return to you later to create a plan that will work for both of us."

REFLECTION

Rewrite your compass statement below (see Chapter 2, page 16). It's important to remember what you wrote. It will guide you on a bad day when you feel like nothing is working. When you want to scream, throw your hands in the air, and give up, your compass statement will keep you moving forward.

____

____

____

____

Did you use one of the scripts in Chapter 6? How did your conversation with your child go?

____

____

____

Tell a trusted friend how it went. They may give you some much-needed encouragement like, "Keep holding on. It's going to get better. You're doing a good job!" Or they may give you some insight that you had not considered before.

____

____

____

What parental changes would you like to make based on your information so far?

____

____

____

CHAPTER 7

Connecting the Dots

At first, I (Katie) had difficulty remaining calm when my daughter didn't attend school. It disrupted my work day. I had to cancel appointments and forgo my exercise. I didn't have the creative energy to follow through on long-term projects.

This left me angry and frustrated.

I'd go upstairs, see my daughter lying in bed, and feel like this whole school refusal situation was a manipulative tactic. I couldn't understand why my daughter went to school some days and not others.

However, I distinctly remember one turning point conversation.

It was probably 9:30 a.m., well past school time. I went upstairs, and my daughter came into the room while I was brushing my teeth and plopped down on the bed. I was more willing to sit beside her because I had already canceled my meetings and wasn't pressed for time.

I stroked her hair and gently asked, "Sweetheart, what's happening? Why don't you want to go to school?"

My daughter could sense my calm and willingness to listen. She began to share her intimate thoughts with me. I learned that inappropriate comments from her peers and teacher had negatively affected her.

I realized how emotionally devastating it was for my daughter to attend school. It was a place where she felt lonely for eight hours every day and struggled academically. I could see this wasn't a manipulative tactic as I had originally thought. She was trying to cope with fear. Fear that was real. Fear that only she could see and feel.

By setting a calm atmosphere and listening with fresh ears, I slowly began to connect the dots.

Some of my daughter's triggers before a day of missed school included:

- Fights with friends

- Dismissive or inappropriate words from teachers

- Long-term assignments that she hadn't started

- My husband's absence due to work travel

- Though I hate to admit it, I also noticed a correlation between incidences of school refusal and nights when my husband and I argued.

Once I connected the dots, I changed the story I'd been telling myself. Laziness, manipulation, and stubbornness weren't the root cause of the school refusal.

When I slowed down and investigated what was happening, I realized that my daughter could overcome school refusal if she had more coping skills to handle the intense emotions she felt inside.

Parent Coaching in Real Time

Look at the information you have so far.

- Did your child provide a reason why they are not going to school?

- What causes have you found during your investigations in Chapters 5 and 6?

Identify at least three triggers. (See the list of external and internal triggers below)

Share with your child what you've noticed.

Say:

> "I've noticed three factors that keep you from wanting to attend school or stay in class. Here they are. Do you agree? Which one affects you the most? Let's take ten minutes to come up with at least one thing we can do to change the situation."

Examples of External Triggers

The night before:

- Went to bed late
- Didn't prepare outfit or bookbag
- Got in a fight with a friend

- Didn't do homework
- Didn't have a conversation to process the day
- Parent traveling out of town
- Parents had a fight
- Change of evening routine
- Domestic violence (physical or verbal)
- Extreme fatigue
- Didn't take medication
- Parent outside the home didn't call or visit
- Other_______________________________

The morning of:

- Didn't sleep well (nightmare or anxious thoughts)
- Didn't sleep long enough
- Got up late
- Not feeling well
- Outfit or hair doesn't "look right"
- Fight with a sibling or parent
- Parents fighting
- Didn't get homework completed
- Didn't eat
- Other_______________________________

At school:

- Boring activity
- Fights with friends
- Failing a subject or test
- Exclusion from activities

- Reprimanded in front of class
- A disapproving look from a teacher
- Bullying
- Watching a peer get bullied
- Unpleasant teacher or subject
- Asking for and not receiving academic or social support
- Embarrassing moments
- Sitting alone at lunch
- Other_____________________________________

Now, it's time to chat about your child's emotions during triggering situations or environments. For example, when a parent outside the home doesn't call. How does your child feel when that happens? Depressed? Angered? Circumstances like this example prompt feelings that cause your child to resist going to school, so have a conversation with your child about their feelings.

Show them the list below. Say to your child, "Let's look at this list of emotions. Check off the ones you experience during difficult situations. What happens to you? What type of things do you say to yourself? Where do you start feeling stress in your body?"

We, as parents, must understand our child's inner happenings (aka emotions) to connect the dots effectively.

If your child isn't willing to do this exercise with

you, we encourage you to complete the checklist to the best of your ability. Use all the information you know and have observed so far.

Examples of Emotions: Internal Happenings

- disappointment
- fear
- shame
- sadness
- anger
- depressed
- worry
- anxiety
- disgust
- lonely
- rejected
- inadequate
- neglected
- helpless
- Other______________________________

REFLECTION

It's time to do some more mindless writing! Remember, it's the best way to get out of your head and move into what's in your heart without anyone judging you.

1. Set a 30-second timer.

2. Close your eyes.

3. Write without lifting your pen for the entire duration.

4. Explore how you feel and what you have been telling yourself.

Prompt:

When I think about my child and his/her/their resistance to school, I...

____

____

____

____

____

CHAPTER 8

Celebrating Your Herculean Effort

For months, I (Katie) felt like I was in a never-ending battle. Despite the changes my husband and I made, the school refusal challenge persisted. I was frustrated, embarrassed, and stressed by everything going wrong.

I learned I needed to focus on what was going well if I wanted to stay motivated.

I needed to celebrate!

I was making progress:

- Instead of yelling or making threats, I was remaining calm.

- Instead of enabling my daughter's moods, I was listening without disdain.

- Instead of waiting till the morning, we had conversations the night before to plan for the next day.

These parenting changes strengthened my relationship with my daughter. And watching me change helped her believe that she could, too.

One day, I was shocked when she said, "I love you, Mom. Thank you for helping me."

Parent Coaching in Real Time

Answer the questions on the reflection page in this chapter. They are important.

1. Take a moment to reward yourself for slowing down and beginning to create supportive boundaries.

2. We want to cheer you on. So drop us an email to brag about yourself. Really! Send us an email at SchoolRefusalSuccess@gmail.com.

REFLECTION

1. What have you done that's made you proud since you began reading this book?

____

____

____

____

2. What's been going well?

____

____

____

3. What positive things have you done or said that you want to keep repeating?

____

____

____

____

4. What small thing can you do to celebrate all the effort you've put in so far?

____

____

____

Take a moment to do a simple, well-deserved victory dance or sing a victory song. Mixing fun with your celebrations will help you keep your spirits up and motivate you to keep going.

If you can't think of anything, do a web search for "ways to reward myself without food or money." You can also look in the Appendix for *7 Ways to Practice Self-Celebration.*

Accountability is important, so make a promise to yourself:

I will celebrate my efforts by ____________________.

I will do this activity before the date of ____________.

CHAPTER 9

Creating a Plan at Home

Once I (Katie) understood the triggers for my daughter's school refusal, I had much more compassion for her. But I made a mistake. I started to believe my daughter was fragile and couldn't cope with the discomfort at school, so I allowed her to stay home when she didn't want to go to school.

I even made home a more cozy, warm, and fun place. We'd make lunch together, and I would let her stay in bed with her iPad. I thought this would be okay as long as she kept up with the work at school. I thought I was protecting her from bullying, academic struggles, and friendship conflicts she experienced at school.

It wasn't until my husband stayed home one morning and observed what was happening that I understood my role in contributing to the problem.

My husband shared his observations with me. That wasn't an easy conversation to have. I became defensive and blamed my husband for traveling and leaving me alone to care for our daughter.

He and I were stuck.

We needed to get on the same page, so with the help of our DBT therapist, we developed a plan.

The first step we had to take was to ensure our daughter wanted and was willing to attend school. We suggested homeschooling or online schooling as options, but our daughter decided she wanted to attend school. This was an essential step as she was making the decision herself. She knew it was what she wanted.

The second step we took was to explicitly communicate our expectations now that she had decided to continue with traditional schooling. She, my husband, and I worked as a team to create natural consequences – both rewarding and deterrent.

Here are the natural consequences we established in our home:

- When my daughter went to school on time, she got an extra hour of iPad time after school.

- When she went late, she only got an extra 30 minutes.

- When she didn't go to school, there was no iPad during the time she was supposed to be at school and no extra iPad time after school.

Lastly, we needed to mitigate the triggers that were causing her not to want to go to school.

My husband stopped traveling for a while, and we put our total effort into supporting our daughter.

He and I made it off-limits to yell during our disagreements and chose to use more productive behavior, like taking a break and addressing issues later when our tempers had cooled down.

We stayed consistent with bedtime routines and wake-up times, and we problem-solved our daughter's outfit and hairstyle ideas the night before.

The last thing we did was to make our home the least desirable environment possible on days my daughter didn't go to school. I wouldn't provide comforting food, extra attention, or give in to iPad or phone requests. I would even turn off the internet if I needed to. Making my home super boring helped.

Parent Coaching in Real Time

Consider what you are willing to do to change your home environment. Make a coping plan together so you know what to do when your child doesn't want to go to school.

Get Clear

Have your child write out their response to the following question.

- What will you do to keep yourself moving on days when you don't want to go to school?

  Child's response: I will ___________________, _________________, and ________________ to make sure I don't give in to the feeling of wanting to stay home.

Write your response to the following question.

- Ask your child, "What would you like me to do on days when you struggle to get up and go?"

  Parent's response: I agree to _____________, _____________, _____________ when I see that you are struggling to go to school.

Set Supportive Boundaries

Use conditional language to communicate the natural consequences, both rewarding and deterrent.

Example: *When* you go to school, *then* you can go to your friend's house.

It works best when your child can help decide on the rewarding consequence. This is the thing that keeps them motivated to go to school.

Example: *When* you choose not to go to school, *then* you will not participate in your next soccer practice or use your device.

Letting your child determine the deterrent consequence is also an excellent idea. Children often choose a harsher outcome than their parents would set. If your child does this, you can let them know you aren't trying to punish them. Your goal is to set supportive boundaries.

Create Stronger Bonds

Prioritize time with your child doing something *they* enjoy.

You Got This!

It truly does take a Herculean effort. And it can feel like your child is intentionally making your life miserable. But keep going! Be consistent. Little by little, your child's behavior will begin to change.

We know this isn't easy, so we are here to cheer you on through this process. Think of *one* thing that's improved in your parenting, *one* improvement your child has made (no matter how small), or *one* thing you're grateful for. Drop us another email at SchoolRefusalSuccess@gmail.com to brag about yourself!

REFLECTION

Take time to reflect on this chapter. Which section do you need to focus on the most?

- Have a meaningful conversation about school options
- Get clearer about motivations and potential responses
- Set more supportive boundaries
- Create stronger bonds

Notes:

____

____

____

____

____

____

CHAPTER 10

Collaborating with the School

My daughter required me to connect with her differently than I (Katie) had in the past.

The most significant change I made at home was to create a calm environment and stay consistent with natural consequences.

I didn't do this by giving in, yelling, or piling on harsh consequences. Instead, I gave my daughter more opportunities to make her own choices. Surprisingly, she began to make more smart choices than she had before. Kudos to her!

While creating a calm, consistent home environment, I contacted the school.

The first person I called was the school's guidance counselor. Together we created a school-home partnership to support my daughter.

The guidance counselor worked with my daughter's homeroom teacher to determine a non-verbal cue my daughter could use if she needed to take a break from the general education setting to visit the counselor.

My daughter's homeroom teacher met with the special education teacher to ensure she could receive extra academic support while we pursued her educational evaluation.

In addition to these steps, I scheduled regular Zoom check-ins with my daughter's homeroom teacher and school counselor to discuss her academic and social-emotional progress.

At home, I stayed consistent with rewarding consequences for going to school and deterrent ones for when she didn't.

Parent Coaching in Real Time

Your path will differ from Katie's. We're not suggesting you do and say everything she did. You will eventually find a solution that works for your family by determining what changes you are willing to make. It is important to choose changes that are in line with your parenting style.

1. Strengthen your school-home partnership by asking your child's teacher or counselor (whomever your child has a good relationship with) for suggestions you can make at home.

2. Take one suggestion the teacher or counselor recommends and implement it consistently for at least two weeks. Remember, positive changes often take a while to happen.

3. Plan a follow-up time to meet with your child's teachers and guidance counselor to discuss your child's progress in attending school.

4. Acknowledge and appreciate your child's small improvements. It's one of the quickest ways to motivate them to continue moving in the right direction.

You may think, "I'm not going to celebrate my child for attending school. That's what they should be doing!" Yes, you are right. Your child should go to school every day. But the fact is, they aren't! And you can't make them go. Your encouraging words, however, can motivate them to go. Studies show that behavior-specific praise increases children's engagement at school and home.[7]

So here are some things you can say to acknowledge their progress:

- I appreciate your effort to push past the discomfort of going to school. It shows your maturity.

- I noticed you did improve at being responsible for going to school this week. What would you like to do for fun on Saturday?

- Your teacher told me you are honoring the agreement you made during our conference. She and I appreciate what you are doing.

---

[7] https://www.tandfonline.com/doi/full/10.1080/1045988X.2023.2181303

REFLECTION

Write down one change you want to make based on this chapter.

____

____

____

____

Write down one, two, or three encouraging statement(s) you can say to your child that feel genuine to you.

____

____

____

____

Notes:

CHAPTER 11

Learning New Skills

Let me (Katie) rewind to the season when we were deep in school refusal. The story you are about to read is one that I'm telling for the first time. It creates incredible shame for me. I share it with you so you know you're not alone in making parenting mistakes.

My daughter and I had just gotten home from a weekend trip. I wanted to return to my routines, and she wanted to spend more time together.

I was practicing an online yoga class when my daughter came into my room and asked if I could help her make a Spotify playlist.

I blew up.

The rage I felt overwhelmed me. I screamed at my daughter. I can't even remember what I said.

I could tell my anger frightened her. I was losing it. I went downstairs to get a glass of water.

It was quiet.

I went back upstairs. My daughter sat in her sister's bed. I saw how deeply my words had scared her.

That was the moment my life changed. I recognized how profoundly my behavior affected my child.

My daughter's response taught me that I needed to learn new skills to manage my emotions and communicate my needs.

I knew how to do certain things well to cope with my feelings. I knew how to exercise and eat healthily. I knew how to pray and reach out to my friends and family. I didn't know how to set boundaries and communicate what I needed.

So that's where I started.

I journaled about the parenting behaviors that were effective – and the parenting behaviors that weren't – when it came to interacting with my daughter.

I no longer allowed myself to yell or be forceful when mad. Instead, I took a break for 15 to 30 minutes to compose myself and get clear on what I needed to communicate.

I also took enabling off the table. I worked hard to notice when I wasn't following through on a natural consequence because I didn't want to deal with my daughter's blowback.

Instead, I tried to state the natural consequence calmly and walk out, ignoring my daughter's reaction.

Next, I learned which behaviors in my coping toolbox were ineffective.

Yelling, using force, enabling, and eating a pan of brownies didn't help me communicate what I needed or problem-solve a situation. It made the situation worse and often created two problems instead of one.

These behaviors were/are the hardest for me to change because I have used them for many years, and they help me to feel better in the moment. But these behaviors also keep me from being the parent or person I want to be.

Once I knew what my ineffective behaviors were, I started to track them daily. Then I used this knowledge to make small changes.

I got clear on what I expected from my daughter and communicated it.

- Instead of allowing my daughter to keep her phone at night, I reorientated her to a new rule: phones needed to be in my room at 8:30 p.m. each school night. When she did this, she got her phone the following day. If not, I kept the phone until after school the next day.

- When my daughter didn't want to do her chores on Saturday morning, I'd calmly communicate that chores helped the family, so when chores were done, she would get technology. Then I would walk out.

I got clear on my expectations and calmly communicated them. I also stayed consistent even when my husband traveled. I began to feel empowered instead of overwhelmed.

I now had the mental space to support my daughter because I had the coping skills I needed to handle emotionally stressful situations.

A cornerstone of DBT-Child therapy is validation. Parents learn how to validate their child's thoughts and feelings so their child feels seen and understood. Once their child feels understood, the parent can coach them to use skills to get through the intense emotion.

I learned to validate my daughter's thoughts and feelings when she strongly reacted to:

- Fights with friends
- Boredom with a class
- Dismissive or inappropriate words from teachers
- Long-term assignments that she hadn't started
- My husband's absence due to work travel
- Being asked to do something she didn't want to do

For our daughter, these external triggers caused her to feel intense shame, fear, rejection, anxiety, and depression. She avoided school, isolated herself in her room, or became defiant to cope with these intense emotions.

I could see my daughter's behavior; what I needed to do was coach my daughter to use more effective coping skills to get through her intense emotions.

In the past, if my daughter woke up in the morning and said, "I'm not going to school today," I would have told her, "Yes, you are, or you are not getting your iPad after school."

Now, however, I validate the thoughts or feelings she may be experiencing by saying, "So you feel lousy and don't feel like attending school today?"

In the past if my daughter called during the school day and said, "Mom, come pick me up, I can't be here," I would have told her, "Ok, I'll come pick you up."

Now I say, "So it feels intolerable right now; what's happening?"

Validation helped me step into my daughter's shoes so that I wasn't minimizing her experience or claiming what she experienced wasn't true.

Once we had a calm atmosphere, she could use coping skills to deal with her emotions about a situation.

One of the most valuable DBT skills for our daughter was willingness.

The willingness skill involves doing what works even if you don't like how it feels. The opposite of willingness is willfulness. Willfulness means staying miserable or using less effective behavior to cope with intense emotions.

This skill helped our daughter get out of bed even when she didn't feel like it. She slowly started recognizing that staying in bed wasn't what she wanted. What she wanted was to be at school and not to feel so lousy.

The more she practiced her willingness to get out of bed, the stronger this behavior became.

Once she got out of bed, she could problem-solve how to cope with the intense feelings triggered by school.

For example, if she didn't want to go to school because all her friends had dropped her, she would exercise her willingness to get out of bed, communicate her feelings to us, and problem-solve the solution.

I might coach her by saying, "OK, so when you feel alone in the hallway or at lunch, what can you do?"

She devised her own solution: to use her earbuds in the hallway and at lunch to distract from her painful thoughts when she felt excluded by her friends.

One day I was surprised when I asked my daughter what helped her the most in getting back to school.

Do you know what she said?

She said, "Watching you and Dad not get mad at each other."

I was floored because I had no idea how much she was learning from watching us change.

She could see my husband and me:

- taking a break instead of yelling
- staying consistent instead of enabling
- prioritizing time together instead of doing our own thing

Our small changes helped our daughter be willing – and brave enough – to go to school even on days she didn't want to. I felt proud of us, and I felt proud of her.

Parent Coaching in Real Time

Here's a script to help you determine if your child is willing to tough it out and continue going to the same school or if they are passionate about going to another. You've got to show your child that you care about what they are experiencing, even if you can't offer them another option right now.

First, you'll say, "Would you want to stay at your school if we could put our minds together to figure out what to do to make school better for you?"

Pause and listen.

Then say, "OK, I'm going to see if I understand. I might not get it right, but please correct me."

Determine if they are willing to do hard things so that they can continue at their current school or if they just want to go to another school.

Having a conversation about alternative options for schooling is tricky. Every family has circumstances that may or may not allow them to change schools, homeschool, or select a private school, charter school, or boarding school.

So how can you have a conversation that doesn't set your child up for disappointment?

Here are five steps to help you have a productive conversation:

1. I see
2. I empathize
3. I don't want

4. I do want
5. I can

1. **I see** how much you are struggling to enjoy school.

2. **I understand**, based on what I know so far, that you don't like going to school because.... Is there anything else that I don't understand? Please explain.

3. **I don't want** to see you struggle for eight hours every day. It pains me to see you so unhappy. I care about you.

4. **I want** you to enjoy school. Believe me, if I could, I would send you to a school that you really like because I want you to be happy.

5. **I can** spend time with you looking at alternative school options that would be best for you. You may wonder why I want us to look at other options if we can't pursue them right now. That's a fair question! Here's the reason.

I want to know what would excite you if I sent you to your ideal school. This will help me better understand what's important to you. Even if I can't change your school right now, I want to start putting a plan in place to improve the current situation and to plan for next school year.

I can't make any promises. But let's come up with a few creative alternatives.

Note: It's essential that you listen to the slightest bit of information your child gives you. Come up with something that shows you listened and are willing to make a small change, even if a big one isn't possible.

CHAPTER 12

Finding Hope on a Bad Day

Once my daughter felt supported at home and school, she regularly went to school. It took a while for me to stop worrying that she wouldn't make it out the door. I had to stop nagging her. She needed to feel that I trusted her to be responsible and independent.

When I stopped worrying, I finally felt normal again! I returned to working full time, creating and managing long-term projects. I felt a sense of creativity I hadn't felt in months. Our daughter felt determined and proud going to school. I thought this would never change.

And then my husband started traveling again. This coincided with my daughter's English project and feeling left out at school – a perfect storm. My daughter started missing school again.

I didn't recognize the waves going on inside her. I only saw her crying, feeling discouraged with her outfit, and refusing to leave the bed in the morning.

I felt anger and fear. I thought, "This wasn't supposed to happen. I thought we were over it!"

I had to remember to go back to what I knew worked:

- set a calm atmosphere

- clearly communicate rewarding and deterrent consequences

- stay consistent even if there was blowback

Initially, I tried to set a calm atmosphere by validating the thoughts and feelings she could be experiencing.

I would say, "So you feel like you don't want to go to school today?" And, "It sucks going to school on days when you don't feel like it."

After that, I would coach her to use the willingness skill to get out of bed: "Sweetheart, you can do this. Exercise your willingness to get out of bed, and let's problem-solve what's happening."

If that didn't work, then I would communicate rewarding and deterrent consequences in the calmest tone possible: "Remember, when you go to school, you get time with your friends and an extra hour of iPad after school. When you stay home, there is no iPad or tech for the rest of the day. You must make up for missed work at school and take an unexcused absence."

And then I would walk out.

Walking out was the hardest for me. I wanted to believe that if I put in more effort, my daughter would go to school, but instead, what I needed to do was pull back.

Pulling back required me to change my mindset. I had to believe that my daughter could navigate difficult situations independently. All she needed from me was to remain calm, coach life skills, and stay consistent with natural consequences.

With this realization, I had hope.

I had hope because I wasn't confused, yelling, or piling on punishments. I had a plan and knew what to do. More importantly, my child was watching me and could see the changes I was making.

Parent Coaching in Real Time

Your child will likely have setbacks, too. But don't be discouraged because there are ways to get back on track.

Here's what you can do:

- Wait until the weekend to address the absence. See if your child can rebound on their own. If they do, be sure to acknowledge this significant improvement.

- If they don't, say, "I noticed you missed school this week more than last week. What changed?"

- Work with your child to come up with commitment and reward statements.

  1. Say, "Name something you REALLY want." Continue with, "Sometimes it helps if we set a goal for ourselves and celebrate when we achieve it."

  2. Take some time to help your child write a goal.

     For example, "I commit to going to school for five consecutive days. When I do, I want to go to the movies."

3. Have your child write their commitment statement and place it somewhere visible.

REFLECTION

Katie's story illustrates her process of personal growth. As she learned new parenting skills, she began to see the positive change in herself, her child's behavior, and her relationship with her child.

What's your biggest takeaway from Katie's story?

____

____

____

____

What's one behavioral change you are willing to make to help your family thrive again?

____

____

____

What's your child's commitment statement?

What do you find interesting about their statement?

CHAPTER 13

Completing the Project

On the days when things don't go well, we encourage you to see school refusal as a project rather than a problem. Think about group projects at a workplace. They are rarely completed in a straight line from point A to point B. They're usually accompanied by bumps, disagreements, and delays along the way. Things inevitably get messy between coworkers, yet the project gets completed.

So it is with school refusal.

What appears to be a total disaster today can be a significant moment of growth for you and your child when their school refusal is finally over. Keep your head up. Things will get better.

We hope you have seen how school refusal created an opportunity for Katie's relationship with her daughter to grow even stronger. As the intimacy grew between them, Katie could think and respond differently than she had before. The result was evident in her daughter's return to school.

Even better, this process improved her daughter's life skills, allowing her to face challenges at school and home confidently.

We know your story is unique, yet as you continue to follow the guidance in this book, you and your child will experience positive outcomes.

Before you close the book, let's see how far you've come! Take a look back at Chapter 2: What's Your Story?

Answer questions 5-10 again on the final reflection page.

FINAL REFLECTION

Compare your answers with the ones you wrote in Chapter 2.

1. Do you know why your child is struggling? If so, explain.

____

____

____

2. How do you feel about your child's school refusal?

____

____

____

3. What feelings do you think your child is dealing with?

____

____

4. Have you considered getting professional support for your child?

____

____

____

5. Have you considered getting professional support for yourself?

____

____

____

We would love to celebrate you and your child's small and big wins. Send us another email at School-RefusalSuccess@gmail.com.

Remember, progress, no matter the size, should be acknowledged and celebrated. This is how you keep the momentum going. You got this! Keep moving forward.

Appendix

Contents

How to Determine Whether You Need a Therapist or Coach

Therapy is most appropriate when there is a history of tense relationships, trauma, or mental illness within the family. Therapists are equipped to dive deeply into past hurts, behaviors, diagnoses, and coping skills.

Coaching is fitting when a situation arises that is difficult for parents to handle. Each family member learns new skills to address the current problem and develops the confidence to solve future challenges.

Generally speaking, mental health professionals help you learn and grow from information drawn from your past, while coaches help you develop strategies to be successful in your current and future endeavors. It can be very helpful to use both simultaneously.

Where to Find Therapy or Coaching

Ask family, friends, your child's physician, and school officials for recommendations.

Check online and with your insurance provider for additional leads.

Schedule complimentary consultations with two or three providers.

We highly recommend you do at least one full session alone before involving your child in therapy. The provider can then get the background information to determine when best to include your child in the sessions.

Dialectical Behavioral Therapy (DBT)

What is Dialectical Behavioral Therapy?
https://childmind.org/article/dbt-dialectical-behavior-therapy/

Find a licensed DBT therapist through the Linehan Board of Certification
https://dbt-lbc.org/index.php?page=101163

Behavior Specialist & Parent Coach
Sharoya Ham, M.Ed.
Embrace Behavior Change
https://www.embracebehaviorchange.com/

Helpful Parenting Book Recommendations

How to Talk So Teens Will Listen and Listen So Teens Will Talk
Author: Adele Faber and Elaine Mazlish

The Conscious Parent: Transforming Ourselves, Empowering Our Children
Author: Dr. Shefali Tsabary

How to Raise an Adult: Break Free of the Overparenting Trap and Prepare Your Kid for Success
Author: Julie Lythcott-Haims

The Self-Driven Child
Authors: Dr. William Stixrud and Ned Johnson

The Power of Validation
Authors: Karyn D. Hall, PhD, and Melissa H. Cook, LPC

The 5 Love Languages of Teenagers: The Secret to Loving Teens Effectively
Author: Gary Chapman

Managing Gaming and Screen Time

Digital Parenting Coaching
Elizabeth Milovidov, Ph.D., J.D
https://www.digitalparentingcoach.com/

Facebook Parent Community Group
https://www.facebook.com/groups/1156604684361405

Getting Unbored

(for middle & high school students)

Finding enjoyment in school is possible. The key is understanding who is responsible for zapping out boredom. It's the person who is bored. When boredom arises, it's the mind's way of saying, *"I'm feeling disconnected; help me figure out how to reconnect."*

Here are five ways you can help your mind get unbored.

1. **Connect with other students** by looking around to see whom you can help when you get bored. Helping others will actually help you.

2. **Connect with your teachers** before or after class, especially the ones you're not fond of. Dare to ask a question about the content, give them a compliment, or bring them a snack. Connecting with your teacher in a small way can make a big difference in accelerating your interest level in class.

3. **Connect with the content.** Commit to asking three meaningful questions each week. Talk with people in careers that interest you. Ask them what they wished they had known or done differently in certain subjects.

4. **Connect to your creativity and talents.** Take a strengths assessment to see what makes you so unique. The HIGH 5 Test: https://high5test.com/ is a good one. Ask yourself, "How can I use my creativity and strengths to make school/class more interesting?" Only you have the answer to this question.

5. **Connect to meaningful school activities.** If one doesn't exist, create it. What do you like to do? Is it gaming? Create a proposal for an after-school gaming club. They do exist. Put together a creative slide presentation and present it to a school administrator.

7 Ways to Practice Self-Celebration

1. Do something that brings you joy that you haven't done in a while. (This could include calling a friend, doing a puzzle, watching a movie, baking, golfing, or knitting.)

2. With your child's permission, brag about your/your child's accomplishments on social media. (Your friends will be thrilled to learn they aren't the only ones having challenges.)

3. Beautify your office. (Purchase a plant, aromatherapy diffuser, or nice piece of art.)

4. Spend time in nature. (Walk, hike, journal, take photos, kayak, visit a park.)

5. Go somewhere you've never been, like a museum or a restaurant. You could even try going solo!

6. Give yourself permission to "break the rules." (If you're a very routine person, celebration looks like giving yourself permission to miss a meeting, not cook, stay in your pajamas all day, and binge-watch shows.)

7. Go hang out! (This might include doing karaoke or going to an art gallery, concert, or craft market. Look online to see what's happening in your area – you'll be amazed!)